ESSENTIAL 101 TIPS

DOG CARE

Dr. Bruce Fogle DVM, MRCVS

WOULDN'T IT BE GREAT
IF YOU COULD GIVE YOUR DOG A PARASITE UMBRELLA?

Parasites don't wait for puppies to grow up, and you don't have to wait to protect them.

REVOLUTION® (selamectin) is a topically applied flea and heartworm medication that is safe for puppies as young as 6 weeks old. REVOLUTION protects your dog from common parasites including:

Heartworms

Fleas

Flea Eggs

Ear Mites

Sarcoptic Mange Mites

American Dog Ticks

REVOLUTION. Start with it. Stick with it.

revolution
(selamectin)

Important Safety Information:
Do not use on sick, weak, or underweight animals. Use only on dogs 6 weeks and older. Use only on cats 8 weeks and older. Prior to administration, dogs should be tested for heartworms. In cats, side effects may include digestive upset and temporary hair loss at application site with possible inflammation. In humans, REVOLUTION may be irritating to skin and eyes. Wash hands after use. For more information, see the Full Prescribing Information.

zoetis

revolution®
(selamectin)

Caring for your new dog is a major responsibility
and we owe it to our pets to protect and care for them
throughout their lifetime.

You're making a great start by using REVOLUTION®,
a topical medicine that protects your dog
against fleas, heartworm, and other
harmful parasites.

Inside you'll find expert advice on many
aspects of caring for and enjoying the company
of puppies and adult dogs – how to handle and
feed them, train and exercise them, and keep
them healthy all year round.

REVOLUTION the best to start with, the best to
stick with.

By the way, REVOLUTION is also available for cats, too!

London, New York,
Munich, Melbourne and Delhi

Author Dr. Bruce Fogle

Senior Editor Ros Walford
Production Editor Kavita Varma
Production Controller Danielle Smith

This American Edition, 2014
First American Edition, 1995

Published in the United States by
DK Publishing,
345 Hudson Street,
New York, New York 10014

006-171201-Dec/14

ISBN 978-1-4654-1303-1

Printed in China

Discover more at
www.dk.com

ESSENTIAL 101 TIPS

HOW TO CHOOSE A DOG

1 WHY BUY A DOG?

Keeping a dog as a pet is a joy – it will give companionship, amusement, and the incentive to exercise, as well as becoming the focus for a family's affections. But ownership also means responsibilities for many years ahead, so ask yourself first what you can commit. Do you have time to exercise a dog daily? Are you prepared to scoop poop? Are you aware of the long-term costs of dog food, vet care, and kennels, for example?

Show dogs are judged against exacting breed standards

Golden Retrievers are responsive to training and alert, but require plenty of exercise

Bearded Collies make friendly family pets

△ **HOUSE PET**
A family dog provides constant companionship and affection in the home.

◁ **SHOW DOG**
Do you want to show your dog? This can become an all-consuming activity as the dog has to be immaculately groomed and totally trained, with all vaccinations up to date.

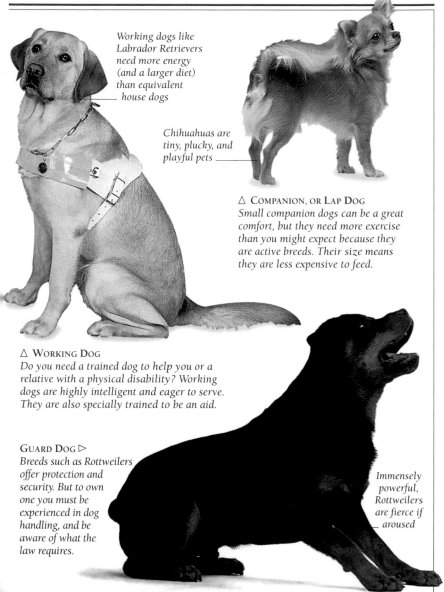

Working dogs like
Labrador Retrievers
need more energy
(and a larger diet)
than equivalent
house dogs

Chihuahuas are
tiny, plucky, and
playful pets

△ COMPANION, OR LAP DOG
Small companion dogs can be a great
comfort, but they need more exercise
than you might expect because they
are active breeds. Their size means
they are less expensive to feed.

△ WORKING DOG
Do you need a trained dog to help you or a
relative with a physical disability? Working
dogs are highly intelligent and eager to serve.
They are also specially trained to be an aid.

GUARD DOG ▷
Breeds such as Rottweilers
offer protection and
security. But to own
one you must be
experienced in dog
handling, and be
aware of what the
law requires.

Immensely
powerful,
Rottweilers
are fierce if
aroused

2 WHY BUY A PEDIGREE?

Pedigree breeds come with documentation, just like automobiles, and there is also plenty of information about their size, feeding, and energy requirements, as well as temperament. Buy a pedigree from a recognized breeder, and check it has a certificate of its lineage and a vaccination record.

BE AWARE
Know what to expect with a pedigree like this Basenji.

3 CROSS-BRED OR RANDOM-BRED?

Not everyone can afford a pedigree, so you are left with a choice between cross-bred or random-bred dogs. As its name suggests, a cross-bred dog is the offspring of two pure-bred dogs and often combines the better traits of both parents. Random-bred dogs are further removed from pure-bred dogs than cross-breds; the randomness of their breeding means such dogs are less likely to suffer from inherited diseases and disabilities than pure-bred dogs.

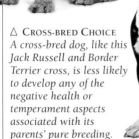

△ **CROSS-BRED CHOICE**
A cross-bred dog, like this Jack Russell and Border Terrier cross, is less likely to develop any of the negative health or temperament aspects associated with its parents' pure breeding.

◁ **RANDOM-BRED CHOICE**
It can be very difficult to determine how big a random-bred puppy will grow, since it comes from such mixed parentage.

4 COATS TO CONSIDER

Coat type is a critical consideration when choosing a dog. Some breeds' coats require daily grooming; with others, bathing can be a chore, as can keeping shed hair off chairs and sofas.

◁ **LONG & SILKY**
Long-coated dogs like the Afghan Hound need daily combing and a regular trim.

△ **SMOOTH COAT**
Smooth, short-haired coats are the easiest to maintain with weekly brushing, as with the Doberman.

◁ **CURLY COAT**
Non-shedding, curly coats, as on this Kerry Blue Terrier, must be clipped every two months.

△ **WIRY COAT**
The stiff, dense hair of an Airedale Terrier requires regular hand-stripping or clipping.

5 WHICH SEX?

Choosing between a male dog or bitch can be difficult, but remember:
- Young unneutered males can be a nuisance when around females in heat.
- Bitches come into "heat" twice a year and this demands extra care.
- Owning a bitch means unwanted pregnancies and male dog attention.

6 A PERFECT PUPPY?

A dog is for life, and opting for a puppy could mean sharing the next 14 years with your pet. Choose a puppy over eight weeks old that appears bright and alert.

△ **LIFT UP TO CHECK UP**
A healthy puppy is happy to be picked up and should feel firm and heavier than you expect. If it relaxes when lifted, this might indicate an easygoing adult-to-be. Observe the puppy in its litter: this can show you its likely temperament.

1 Lift the ear flaps to see if the ear is pink inside, with neither an unpleasant odor nor any obvious sign of crusty or waxy discharge. Such deposits or discharges might indicate ear mites. Check that the ear flaps hang evenly. Some head and ear shaking is normal, especially after waking.

2 To check teeth and gums, gently part the lips. See that the gums and tongue are pink (or mottled with black pigment), and odor-free. Gums should form a clean margin with the teeth. In most breeds (the Boxer is an exception), the teeth should generally meet perfectly in a scissor bite.

A PUPPY'S FUR SHOULD BE SHINY

3 Hold the head still and check that the eyes are clear, bright, and free from any discharge – stains around the facial hair might indicate the latter. There should be good pigmentation and no sign of redness, squinting, or inflammation. A puppy that paws at its eyes may have an irritation.

4 Check for oily or flaky skin, and make sure there are no sores or lumps. The hair should be firm and not come out when you stroke it (healthy fur glistens and comes out only when shedding). Run your hand against the grain of the coat to help you spot any skin defects or parasites.

5 The anal region under the tail should be clean and dry. There should be no inflammation or sign of diarrhea, dried feces, or other discharge from the genitals. Dragging the rear along the floor or excess licking can often indicate an irritation caused by blocked anal glands.

7 TEST BEFORE YOU BUY

If you decide to purchase a mature dog over six months old, do not go just on appearances. Before you take it away, try to test its temperament by seeing if it seems willing to obey and to respond to commands, accepts being touched, is not hand-shy or nervous in any way, and also does not bark at every opportunity.

GAUGE A DOG'S RESPONSE TO TRAINING
Will the dog sit on command? If it refuses to sit, tuck it into a sitting position to see how it might then respond to your voice and physical presence.

8 WHERE TO BUY

First ask your vet for sources. Animal shelters are another source but the dog may take time to settle down. Look also in your local paper.

9 TAG YOUR DOG

In many areas the law on dogs dictates that you must have an identity tag on your dog's collar.

Inside data

ROLL TAG
The owner and dog details go on a paper roll inside the tag.

BRASS TAG
Practical and designed to last.

10 VET CHECK

Ask pet-owning friends to recommend a vet. Visit the office to see if the place suits your needs, and to discuss your dog's vaccinations, diet, worming, and checkups.

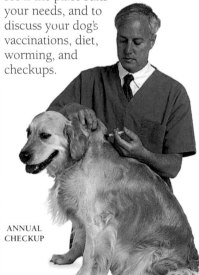

ANNUAL CHECKUP

FIRST HANDLING

11 CARRYING A PUP

Accustom your puppy or small dog to being picked up and carried. Reassure it first, especially a small dog, before trying to pick it up. Aim to hold the animal firmly, but comfortably, and stop it from squirming and paddling. The grasp shown here will prevent jumping.

CORRECT HOLD FOR PUPPY/SMALL DOG
Place one hand under the small dog's or puppy's forelimbs and chest. Put the other hand around the hind limbs and rump for firm control. Lift your dog in this position.

PUPPY FEELS SAFE AND COMFORTABLE

12 PICKING UP A LARGE DOG

Even large dogs must be lifted occasionally; it is best to teach them this at a young age. Always talk to your dog to reassure it before trying to pick it up. Muzzle it if in any doubt about its temperament. Place one of your arms around the dog's chest and fore-limbs, the other around its rump, then lift it up.

1 Bend your knees, draw the dog to your chest, and straighten your back.

2 Lift it up carefully in a secure grip. Release at once if it starts to panic.

13 COLLAR CHOICE

Collars are made from leather, rope, or supple meshed nylon. Attach an ID tag to the collar. Puppies should wear collars from eight weeks old, but with some supervision at first.

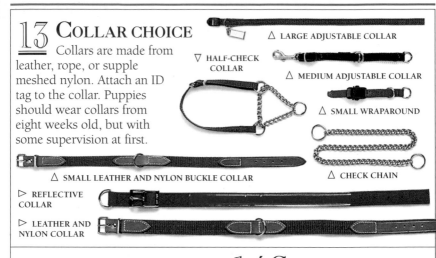

△ LARGE ADJUSTABLE COLLAR

▽ HALF-CHECK COLLAR

△ MEDIUM ADJUSTABLE COLLAR

△ SMALL WRAPAROUND

△ SMALL LEATHER AND NYLON BUCKLE COLLAR

△ CHECK CHAIN

▷ REFLECTIVE COLLAR

▷ LEATHER AND NYLON COLLAR

14 COLLAR IT

Put a puppy's first collar on for short periods each day so it grows used to it. Remove the collar when you cannot supervise the puppy. As the dog grows in size, check the collar size and change as necessary.

1 △ Check the length of the collar around the dog's neck. Make sure it does not catch a long-haired dog's fur.

2 ▷ You should be able to slip two fingers under a well-fitting collar. The collar will not come off if the dog tugs backward on its leash, but can be slipped off without discomfort if needed.

15 HOW TO CHOOSE A LEASH

With a puppy or new dog, start with one long training leash for outdoor training, and a long light houseline with a bolt snap for indoor control. Also, buy one short leash for first walks and early training. Do not use leashes to punish dogs.

◁ 6 FT (2 M) COTTON LEASH

△ EXTENSION LEASH

◁ NYLON-CORD LONG LINE

◁ 20 FT (6 M) COTTON LEASH

△ STANDARD LEATHER LEASH

16 HELP WITH HEAD HALTERS & HARNESSES

A head halter is ideal for a fearful or bold dog and for one that chews too much. Made of strong nylon, it clips onto a leash via a ring under the dog's jaw. If the dog pulls or lunges, its own momentum pulls its head down and its jaws shut. This is an alternative to a check chain.

A harness for small dogs slips over the body and around the chest. The leash is attached over the dog's back to avoid collar pressure on the neck.

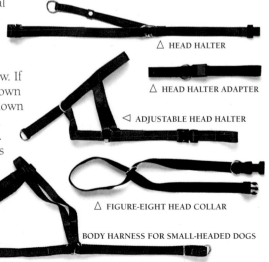

△ HEAD HALTER

△ HEAD HALTER ADAPTER

◁ ADJUSTABLE HEAD HALTER

△ FIGURE-EIGHT HEAD COLLAR

BODY HARNESS FOR SMALL-HEADED DOGS

17 PUTTING ON A HEAD HALTER

A large dog that could become difficult to control in public will be more responsive to a head halter.

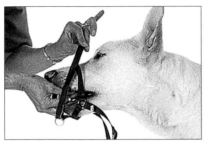

1 Slip a strong, nylon head halter over the dog's mouth, putting your hand under its jaw to hold its head up.

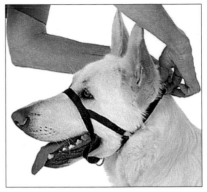

2 Fasten the halter behind the dog's neck. Make sure it is not tight: you should be able to slip two fingers under it.

18 SAFE STEPS TO MUZZLE YOUR DOG

Where the law or common sense about bite prevention dictates, make sure your dog wears a muzzle.

1 Kneel by your dog and strap on the muzzle, starting from under its chin. Pull the straps behind gently and fasten.

2 Make sure the muzzle fits securely, but that it is not too tight. The dog should be able to open its jaws and pant.

19 HANDLING WITH A CHECK CHAIN

When out walking, especially if there are children around, and for boisterous breeds with short attention spans, a check chain or a half-check collar is ideal for sure control.

1 Hold the check chain open in a circle and gently slip it over the dog's head. It should hang loosely around its neck.

Dog responds to half-check collar

HALF-CHECK COLLAR
Pull up on the leash to tighten. This gives firm control over aggression.

2 In the correct position, as shown, it will tighten only when tension is applied. Keep the dog on your left side.

INCORRECT METHOD
If the chain is put on backward it will cause discomfort and will not loosen.

20 BEDDING DOWN

Set up the dog bed in a busy part of the home, such as a kitchen corner. A bean bag can make a light, soft bed that retains body heat and is easy to wash, or consider a chewproof plastic basket with a well-fitting washable mattress: it is harder-wearing and easier to clean than a wicker version.

A SECURE PLACE TO WATCH THE FAMILY

21 PUPPY PEN FOR PEACE OF MIND

It is worth buying a secure puppy pen, with an open top, for a new, untrained dog. Ensure it has:

- Newspaper to soak up accidents.
- Fresh water and a chew toy.
- A comfortable basket or bean bag.

Always leave fresh water

Puppy can watch house activity

Newspaper for toilet training

Toy for stimulation

HEALTHY FEEDING

22 THE BEST BOWLS

A dog must have its own feeding bowl. For durability, buy your dog a stainless steel bowl, with the bottom rimmed with rubber to prevent sliding. A heavy ceramic bowl can't be knocked over easily, but if it chips or cracks replace it, since bacteria will breed there.

Ceramic bowl

Puppy bowl

Stainless steel bowl

23 HOW MUCH WATER?

Make sure your dog has fresh water available, and replenish to the same level daily. A dog loses water every day in urine, feces, and through panting. Your dog could suffer from irreversible body dehydration and damage if water is not available for over 24 hours.

Keep the water bowl clean and refill it daily

24 SIMPLE STEPS ON HOW AND WHEN TO FEED

You can give an adult dog (generally over nine months old) its daily food allowance in one meal; or you can split the same amount into two meals.

- Small dogs have smaller stomachs and eat less in one meal. Therefore, to help its digestion, feed a small dog on a twice daily basis.
- Puppies need three or more meals a day, reduced to two when they reach six months old. From six to nine months of age you can start to introduce adult dog food.
- Treat a sick dog as you would a puppy, giving it three small meals a day. Seek the advise of your veterinarian if your dog refuses to eat.
- Pregnant bitches need up to 50 per-cent more food. Consult a vet on any special dietary needs.

- Make sure the basic diet includes protein for growth and tissue repair.
- Check for essential fatty acids to give a glossy sheen to a dog's coat.
- Look for carbohydrates in the ingredients, to provide bulk and help your dog's bowel movements.
- Little and often is a good rule for older dogs. Over 12 years of age food becomes a daily highlight.
- Always be sure to serve your dog's meal at room temperature.
- Never offer stale or spoiled food.
- Never feed processed cat food to your dog: it is too high in protein.
- Remove canned or wet food after 10 to 15 minutes, and give a new serving at the next mealtime.
- If your dog refuses to eat for 24 hours consult your vet.

Daily requirements for normal adult dog (*approximate guide only*)

Dog weight/type	Calories needed	Canned food	Premium dry food	Commercial dry food
Very small: 11 lb/5 kg Yorkshire Terrier	210	⅓–1 can	¼–1¼ cups	⅓–1¼ cups
Small: 22 lb/10 kg Cairn Terrier	590	1–2 cans	1¼–1¾ cups	1¼–2¼ cups
Medium: 44 lb/20 kg Springer Spaniel	900	2–3 cans	1¾–3½ cups	2⅓–3⅔ cups
Large: 88 lb/40 kg German Shepherd	1,680	3–6 cans	3½–5 cups	4¼–5⅓ cups
Giant: 176 lb/80 kg Great Dane	2,800	1 can per 15 lb body weight	5 cups + ½ per 15 lb over 100 lb	6⅔–9 cups

25 DECIDING ON FRESH FOOD

Meat provides most, but not all, of a dog's daily nutritional needs. However, like humans, dogs cannot live on meat alone, so if you are going to feed your dog fresh food rather than prepared foods, make sure to mix the meat with the correct amount of cereals, vegetables, pasta, and rice to provide all the protein, carbohydrates, fat, vitamins, and minerals it needs for good health. The nutrient content of fresh meat varies considerably, so keeping a consistently balanced diet can be quite difficult.

MEAT AND VEGETABLES
All your dog's nutritional needs are in this dish.

HIGH-FAT GROUND MEAT
A major source of calories, with a high level of fat.

LOW-CALCIUM LIVER
Rich in vitamins A, B₁, high phosphorus, low calcium.

HIGH-CALORIE HEART
High fat content; double the calories of kidney.

LOW-CALORIE CHICKEN
Easily digested and lower in calories than other meats.

LIGHT SCRAMBLED EGG
Nonmeat nutrition for very young and recuperating dogs.

ENERGY-GIVING PASTA
Good carbohydrate source, but may require flavoring.

23

26 VEGETABLES FOR DOGS

Uncooked vegetables (and certain raw fruits) are good sources of vitamins. Dogs are not total meat-eaters and can convert vegetable protein and fat into the nutrients necessary to survive. Choose freshly cooked vegetables, such as carrots, cabbage, and potatoes, as part of a well-balanced diet. If you want to put your dog on a vegetarian diet, consult your vet about how to maintain balanced nutrition.

VITAMIN-RICH MIXED VEGETABLES

27 COMPLETE DRY FOODS

These almost odorless meat and fish pellets have four times as many calories per pound as canned food, so feed in smaller quantities. Some types must be rehydrated with water. Do not confuse these complete meals with snack-based, mainly cereal dog-meals or cookies.

REHYDRATED

FOR SENIOR DOG

LOW-CALORIE

HIGH-ENERGY

STANDARD DRY

28 COMPLETE SEMIMOIST FOOD

Complete semimoist food has more than three times the calories of canned food and makes an excellent prepared pet meal. It provides a complete and economical diet, and you can give it to your dog by itself or with a cereal filler. It has a high carbohydrate content suitable for working dogs – but not for diabetic dogs. It also tends to have a shorter shelf life than dry or canned food.

SEMIMOIST MEAL

29 CANNED FOOD CHOICE

Meaty, high-protein, canned foods come in many varieties to suit different dog owners' requirements. The main variety is a chunks in gel mix, best given to your dog with an equal volume of cereal filler or crunchy dry food to insure a good level of calories, carbohydrates, and fat. Some canned foods are prepared for dogs with finicky appetites and can be fed without dry food, still giving a dog enough nutrients.

CHUNKS IN GEL

30 STORING FOOD

MADE-TO-MEASURE PLASTIC LIDS

Put a plastic lid on top of a partly used can of dog food, and store in a refrigerator for a maximum of three days. Wash the lids after use separately from the family cutlery – as you would wash the dog's bowls and serving spoon.

31 VITAMINS & MINERALS

Your dog should get all the vitamins and minerals it requires from either the fresh meat, cereals, vegetables, or prepared pet foods you give it. However, there are certain times when a dog may require supplements to insure bone growth, good digestion, tissue repair, water balance, and other conditions. These times include pregnancy, puppy growth, and when a dog is recuperating from injury or illness. If your pet is in such a condition, talk to your vet about the level of supplement needed before adding any to its diet.

VITAMIN TABLETS
Dispense only as directed by your vet.

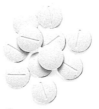

CALCIUM
Essential for puppies and pregnant and lactating bitches.

BONE MEAL
An extra source of calcium: buy it sterilized.

32 BONES OR CHEWS?

Bones for chewing help to supply vital calcium, but if you feed your dog a balanced diet it will be receiving enough calcium already. Gnawing on bones massages the gums and exercises the jaw muscles. Beef shin or knuckle bones are best since they are less likely to splinter when gnawed or to stick in the mouth. Bones are dangerous for some dogs. Consult a vet before providing them. Chews are an effective and more convenient alternative, with fewer calories.

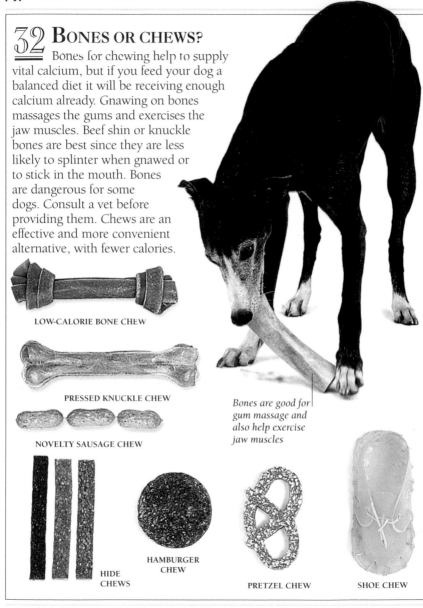

LOW-CALORIE BONE CHEW

PRESSED KNUCKLE CHEW

NOVELTY SAUSAGE CHEW

Bones are good for gum massage and also help exercise jaw muscles

HIDE CHEWS

HAMBURGER CHEW

PRETZEL CHEW

SHOE CHEW

33 TIDBITS & TREATS

Off-the-shelf cookies, chunks, and rings make tasty snacks and are useful training rewards. Such treats are high in carbohydrates and fat, which means high calories, so take them into account when considering your dog's daily calorie intake.

WHOLE GRAIN

MINI-MARROWBONE

MIXED FLAVORS

BACON-FLAVORED

CHICKEN STRIPS

BEEF BONES

BEEF SOFT CHUNKS

SAVORY RINGS

34 WEIGHT WATCH FOR DOGS

If your dog is less alert than usual, and if you also cannot feel its ribs, you may be overfeeding it or feeding it incorrectly.

- Aim to give your dog only 60 percent of its normal recommended calorie allowance during dieting.
- Reduce a dog's dry food intake if feeding it a meat and dry food mix.

- Increase the dog's daily exercise.
- Vary the diet from time to time.
- Do not give in to begging for food: this can be an obsession with some dogs, especially if they are bored. Surrendering just reinforces this behavior and leads to obesity.
- Consult your vet about specially formulated, low-calorie diets.

ESSENTIAL EARLY LEARNING

35 USE A NEWSPAPER

If you have a new adult dog that has not been housebroken, treat it just like a new puppy. Puppies relieve themselves every few hours after eating, drinking, waking, or playing. Train your dog to use newspaper indoors, before moving outside.

Sniffs to find spot to urinate

1 ▷ Sniffing the ground is the sure, and often the only, sign that your dog wants to relieve itself. You only have a few seconds to intervene, so have some newspaper ready.

2 Quickly pick up the dog and place it on the newspaper. Newspaper is ideal as it is very absorbent. Then keep checking and stand by to encourage it.

3 If you can, keep some of the soiled newspaper to show the puppy its own odor and to encourage it to use that spot again. Praise your puppy afterward.

36 CRATE-TRAINING ROUTINE

A dog that has been trained from puppyhood to use a crate will see it as a secure haven in a busy area, such as a kitchen. Dogs will not willingly foul their sleeping area, so it is ideal for housebreaking.

- Leave it in the crate when you are busy. Make sure it has soft bedding, a bowl of fresh water, and a chew toy.
- Keep a regular check if it wants to relieve itself, especially after it has just eaten or woken up.
- Do not leave your dog in its crate for more than two to three hours at a time during the daytime.
- Keep a newspaper (see p.28) in view so the puppy comes to recognize this as its first toilet area.

SAFE AND SECURE "HOME"

37 WHEN HOUSEBREAKING FAILS

Your new dog or puppy is bound to have accidents to start with, but never punish it for making a mess in the home. This only makes it more nervous. Nor should you use a crate as a place of discipline: it serves as a home, not a jail, and should be your pet's favorite resting place.

Clean up a messy area with an odor-eliminating disinfectant, because dogs will return to the same smell and defecate there again. Do this quickly as dog droppings are unpleasant and a health hazard. Avoid using ammonia products to clear up because the smell may remind a dog of its own urine.

Wash hands afterward

Disinfectant kills germs

Wear rubber gloves

38 OUTDOOR TRAINING

As soon as possible, train your puppy to relieve itself outside. Start with your yard (where you can remove the feces and flush it away), then go to a suitable public space with a poop scoop. Keep the puppy on a leash until it relieves itself in a specific spot.

1 ▷ Standing by the door is a sign that a dog wants to relieve itself outside.

2 Train your dog to sniff out a remote spot to urinate on. Luckily, dogs like to relieve themselves in specific places.

3 Use words like "hurry up" as it relieves itself; then praise it. Soon your dog will relieve itself on your "hurry up" command.

39 HOW TO POOP-SCOOP

A walk stimulates a dog to defecate, usually within the first ten minutes. Always carry a poop scoop or biodegradable bag, and keep your dog on a leash until it deposits on a suitable spot (give the leash a quick jerk if the site is unacceptable). Afterward, let the dog off the leash. It will soon learn that it has to perform before it can play. Clear up with a poop scoop, or bag, and discard feces.

SPECIFICALLY MADE POOP SCOOP

40 STOP CHEWING!

Puppies chew out of curiosity about the things around them; older dogs delight in chewing objects, such as shoes, which you would not normally allow. Limit chewing to a few chosen objects. In this way your pet will learn to chew only what you give it.

Apply bitter, nontoxic spray on objects it wants but you don't want it to have

CHEWING SHOES
Prevent this bad habit from forming by not allowing your dog to chew even old shoes.

41 STOP STEALING FOOD!

Dogs instinctively look for food; what we think is garbage can be tasty to a dog. Train your pet to feed only from its bowl and make sure you leave all food covered.

- Use a firm verbal "leave" command.
- Put the lid firmly on the can to hide any tempting food morsels.
- Squirt the can with a bitter-tasting spray to make it unpleasant to the dog.

KEEP FOOD OUT OF SIGHT

Refuse to allow it any tidbits from the table

42 STOP BEGGING!

Train your pet to take food only from its bowl, well away from where you eat. Command your dog to "sit," put its bowl on the floor, then say "okay" and allow it to eat.

FIRM COMMAND
Firm body language backs up verbal "sit" command.

Dog makes desire for treat obvious

HOWLS OF BOREDOM
A dog may howl when it is bored or lonely.

43 BARK OFF!

A dog barks to alert and protect its owner but this needs to be controlled. Shouting "quiet!" may only excite it more. For long-term control, practice regularly giving the command "speak" when it starts to bark. Follow this with "quiet" or "no." With training, the dog will learn to "speak" (that is, bark) and to be quiet on your command.

GOOD GROOMING

44 SHEDDING

Smooth and short-haired coats can shed all year and require frequent brushing. Curly and wiry coats shed less; they keep growing, and need regular attention.

45 CLIPS & CUTS

Fast-growing coats need to be clipped or cut, while heavy coats require thinning out. Accustom your pet to a routine (and to the sound of clippers), as a young dog.

46 PREPARE TO GROOM

Position your pet on a nonslip mat at a height where you do not have to bend over for grooming, and insure your scissors, brushes, and combs are ready. Hold the dog with a hand under the belly, and put the thumb of the other hand under its collar.

Hand placed palm down

Antislip mat

Grooming kit ready for use

47 TURN YOUR DOG

If you cannot reach over the back of your dog to groom its coat on the other side, turn it. Place the flat of your hand, with the fingers reasonably close, over the hindleg muscles and bring it around. Keep the palm flat to avoid hurting the dog.

Dog accepts your hands

48 FACE CLEANING

You should inspect your dog's ears, eyes, and teeth once a week. Breeds with skin folds, like this Shar Pei, need extra attention. Daily or weekly routine grooming sessions help keep your pet's face, skin, coat, and nails healthy, and also provide a regular opportunity for you to reinforce your authority and control. If a dog is difficult, start with giving the "sit" and "stay" commands. End each session with verbal praise and reassuring pats.

COTTON BALLS

1 Hold the head firmly with one hand; gently wipe the skin around the eye with the other hand, using a piece of fresh, damp cotton ball. Remove mucus.

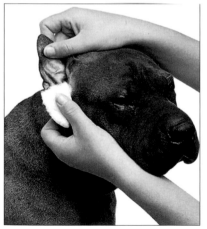

2 With one hand, hold open the ear and gently clean inside the flap with another fresh, wet cotton ball. Try to avoid probing deep into the ear.

3 Some dogs' facial skin forms natural traps for dirt, debris, and dead skin that harbor bacteria. Clean loose skin regularly with a fresh, damp cotton ball.

49 CLEANING TEETH & GUMS

Your dog's teeth should be inspected by a vet at least annually. Once a week, however, you should check that your dog's teeth and gums show no signs of infection. Over 75% of adult dogs require dental attention; the first warning sign is often bad breath caused by bacteria multiplying in food trapped between teeth. If you neglect weekly grooming and an annual vet checkup, removal of teeth may be the only remedy. To prevent tooth decay you can also buy special oral hygiene gels from your local vet. Apply directly as with toothpaste, or mix in with a small amount of food. Do this on average once a week.

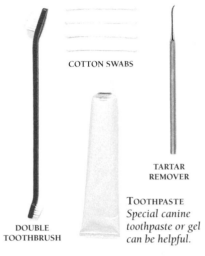

COTTON SWABS

TARTAR REMOVER

TOOTHPASTE
Special canine toothpaste or gel can be helpful.

DOUBLE TOOTHBRUSH

1 Check carefully for dental plaque and hardened tartar. These are caused by bacteria buildup and will lead to bad breath and inflammation of gum tissue.

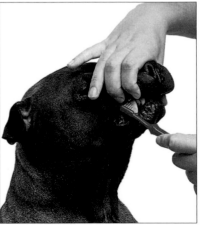

2 Make sure your dog knows you are in command, then gently brush its teeth with a soft toothbrush. Apply special dog toothpaste, gel, or dilute salt water.

50 BATHE YOUR DOG

You may need to bathe your dog to rid it of skin parasites, to alleviate a skin condition, or just if it rolls in something foul! Ask your vet to recommend the appropriate shampoo. Rinse well, as leftover shampoo may cause needless skin irritation.

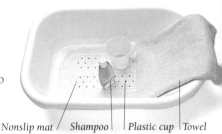

Nonslip mat / Shampoo | Plastic cup | Towel

1 Keep your dog's collar on in the bath to hold the dog and stop it from jumping out. Use a rubber mat in the bath to prevent your dog from slipping. You may also want to plug its ears with a cotton ball. Hold the collar and pour warm water on its coat.

2 Keeping one hand on the collar, use a special canine shampoo to soap the dog all over, except for its head. Work up a good lather, and massage the skin against the lie of the coat. Rub the shampoo well into its coat to loosen dirt and dead skin.

3 Now, use both hands to lather the dog's head, massaging the hair gently. You will not need to hold on to its collar at this stage. Be extremely careful not to splash the eyes with soapy water, and to avoid getting the lather in your pet's mouth.

4 Rinse and dry the dog's head thoroughly before rinsing the body. It is most likely to shake when its head gets wet, so this will stop it from shaking water all over you. Be careful around the ears and eyes, and praise it with encouraging words.

5 Next, rinse the rest of its body using clean, warm water. Make sure you remove all the soap from its coat. Keep rinsing until you are sure the coat is shampoo-free. Massage out any excess water.

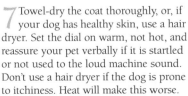

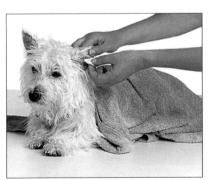

6 When you are sure that you have squeezed out any excess water, dry your dog's coat with a towel and then lift it, wrapped up as much as possible in the towel. Remove the ear plugs and dry the inside of the ears carefully. Always remember to dry well under the collar.

7 Towel-dry the coat thoroughly, or, if your dog has healthy skin, use a hair dryer. Set the dial on warm, not hot, and reassure your pet verbally if it is startled or not used to the loud machine sound. Don't use a hair dryer if the dog is prone to itchiness. Heat will make this worse.

51 TRIMMING NAILS

The best time to trim nails is just after a bath, when the nails are softer than usual. Be careful not to trim the pink area lying inside the nail.

NAIL CLIPPERS

1 △ Spread each of your dog's feet and inspect the area between the toes for dirt and debris. Clean in the recesses with a moistened cotton ball.

2 ◁ Clip your pet's nails carefully using specifically made canine or "guillotine" nail clippers. Smooth over any rough edges with a nail file or emery board.

52 WHERE TO TRIM

The pink area underneath the nail is living tissue with blood and nerves, and is called the quick, or nail bed. You must avoid cutting this tissue when trimming the nails. Cut diagonally down the nail only a fraction of an inch. If in doubt, ask your vet to perform this for you.

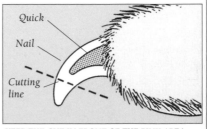

Quick

Nail

Cutting line

KEEP THE CUT IN FRONT OF THE PINK AREA

53 GROOMING A SHORT COAT

Short coats need less grooming than long coats, but some are prone to heavy shedding. To control the hair and dandruff, a daily grooming may be necessary.

BRISTLE   **SLICKER**   **COMB**

1 Use a slicker brush, which is designed to remove tangles and prevent matting (short, dense coats mat easily). With firm, long strokes, brush along your pet's body and tail.

2 Next, use a bristle brush to remove all dead hair and remaining dirt. Brush the entire coat, including tail and legs.

3 Run a fine comb through the feathers on the dog's legs and tail. If there are straggling hairs from the feathers, trim these with scissors. While grooming, check your pet for parasites and sores.

54 Grooming a smooth coat

Smooth-coated dogs such as Boxers are the easiest to groom, and look at their peak with a brush and polish once or twice a week. Use conditioner to help soften the hair.

RUBBER BRUSH   **CHAMOIS**   **BRISTLE BRUSH**

1 Select a rubber brush, and use this first to loosen any dead hair and surface dirt. Work against the lie of the fur to help you loosen the debris.

2 Next, use a bristle brush to remove the dead hair and skin. Make sure you brush the dog's entire coat, including its tail and legs.

3 Polish your pet's coat briskly with a chamois cloth to bring out the shine. You can also apply a coat conditioner to give your dog's coat a glossy sheen.

55 Hand-stripping a wiry coat

Dogs with wiry coats must be hand-stripped every three or four months. Pluck dead hair using your thumb and finger, or thumb and stripping knife, in direction of growth.

STANDARD STRIPPING KNIFE

HAIR PLUCKED BETWEEN THUMB AND KNIFE

56 SUCCESS WITH SILKY COATS

Long coats require more care than short coats. Silky-coated dogs like Yorkshire Terriers have no downy undercoat and need extra care when grooming to avoid scratching the skin.

SLICKER COMB SCISSORS BRUSH

1 Use a slicker brush, specially designed to remove any tangles. Gently tease out the mats, taking special care not to pull on your pet's hair and break it.

2 Groom the coat again, using a bristle brush to bring out the shine. At this stage, the brush should move through the coat with very little resistance.

3 Carefully take the long hair on the dog's back and part down either side of the center using the comb, and then comb each side straight down. You can trim any straggling ends with scissors.

4 Trim carefully around the feet and ears with the scissors. You can trim above the eyes, or tie the hair back with a bow.

Neat and gleaming coat

57 TAKING OUT LONG HAIR TANGLES

Dogs with long coats, such as Rough Collies and Shetland Sheepdogs, also have dense, thick, protective down. If you do not regularly groom your dog's long coat using both a slicker and a bristle brush, it will mat easily, and you will find it difficult to achieve a sleek and tidy coat.

SLICKER **SCISSORS** **COMB** **PIN BRUSH**

1 If you own a long-haired dog such as a Rough Collie, you must give it a daily thorough groom as well as a regular, but less frequent, trim. Start with a slicker brush and gently untangle your pet's matted hair and knots. Avoid being too vigorous when you brush the coat.

2 Run a pin brush through your dog's coat. To avoid pulling out the hair, do not do this too vigorously. There should be no large tangles left. Long-haired dogs with thick coats can get mats under their legs: take extra care when grooming these areas, where the skin is usually more sensitive.

3 Comb through the hair with a wide-toothed comb, to break up any leftover small tangles. Follow this with a finer comb. Good-quality steel, wide-toothed and fine-toothed combs are essential for removing tangles, mats, and debris from thicker, longer hair. Do not use short bristle brushes.

4 Trim the long hair around your dog's feet with a pair of sharp scissors. Remember to trim between the toes, where dirt can become lodged and may cause irritation if not removed. Reduce the risk of dirt becoming embedded between the toes by trimming the hair directly after exercise.

5 Trim around the hocks (the central back joint on the hind legs) and feathers (the long, fine fringe of hairs) with the sharp scissors, so that the hair does not become tangled and collect dirt and debris. You should groom a long-haired dog for at least 15 minutes to make the session effective.

TAKING THE LEAD

58 STARTING YOUR DOG'S TRAINING

Dogs have short attention spans, so keep each training session short, and always end it on a positive, encouraging note. Use verbal praise, physical reassurance, and an instant reward to reinforce initial training.

- Always use a leash to insure control.
- Sessions should last no more than 15 minutes, twice a day maximum.
- Cancel if you (or the dog) are tired.
- End each session on a positive note.
- Finish training with a play session.

59 GIVING COMMANDS

You will need to use food rewards at first to reinforce your commands. A hungry dog is alert and ready to respond. Make the treat visible but do not offer your dog any morsel until it carries out a command.

FOOD INDUCED ▷
Effective reward for hungry dog.

Dog sits on command for reward

No offer of food, but verbal praise

Dog sits at verbal command only

△ WORD ENFORCED
Reduce snacks gradually, so the dog reacts solely to your body language and verbal praise.

60 COMMAND YOUR DOG TO SIT

The first and generally easiest commands to teach your new dog or puppy are "sit" and "come."

- Practice control first with a leash.
- Start sessions with a food reward.
- Aim to make it sit by words alone.

Dog responds to food held in front of middle of body

Food held directly above dog's head

1 Facing the dog, move away with the leash in your left hand and treat in your right. Say "come" and show it the treat.

2 As it reaches you, move your right hand up and over its head. It will bend its hind legs as it keeps an eye on the food.

3 Give the command "sit" when you see it about to sit. Then practice again, and from the side. Reduce the treat each time.

61 REFUSING TO SIT

Making your new dog or puppy learn to sit down will take many practice sessions. If it refuses to sit even with a treat, kneel down and hold its collar with your right hand. Tuck its hindquarters under with your left hand and give the command "sit" as you do this. Reward the dog with praise and a treat. Repeat the step, giving just praise alone, until it responds to this.

Fingers kept together in the tuck, to avoid hurting the dog

62 WAIT & COME COMMAND

Making your dog wait, and then come to you when you call it, is known as recall training. An untrained dog is bound to follow you at first, so take it back and repeat the command (*see step 1*).

1 ◁ Place your dog in the sit position and give the command "sit-wait." Avoid the word "stay," which it might confuse with the "stay until I return" command.

2 ▷ Draw the length of the leash away from your dog, face the dog, show a food reward, and call its name, adding the command "come."

Dog moves toward you and the treat

Dog sees food treat in right hand

4 ▽ Now practice the commands over a greater distance, with your dog on a long line. Use a toy reward that your dog can see from a distance, rather than offering a food morsel.

Long line is slack, but can be pulled to ensure compliance

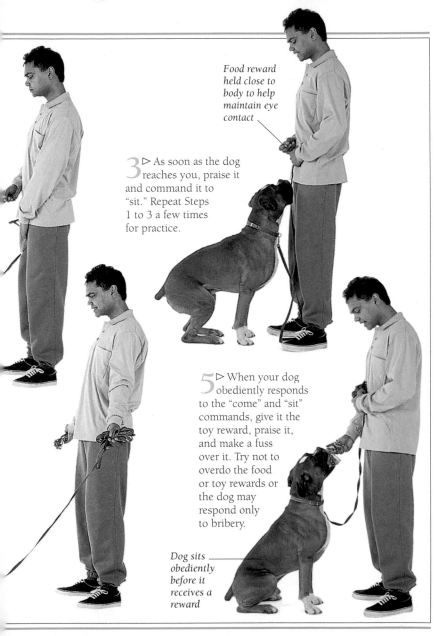

Food reward held close to body to help maintain eye contact

3 ▷ As soon as the dog reaches you, praise it and command it to "sit." Repeat Steps 1 to 3 a few times for practice.

5 ▷ When your dog obediently responds to the "come" and "sit" commands, give it the toy reward, praise it, and make a fuss over it. Try not to overdo the food or toy rewards or the dog may respond only to bribery.

Dog sits obediently before it receives a reward

63 COMMAND TO LIE DOWN

This command teaches the dog that you are in control; it is a good command to use when there are a lot of distractions. There are two lying positions: the "sphinx," where the hind legs tuck under the body, and "flat," where the hips are rolled and the legs are on one side. Either position is natural.

End of leash held secure under knees

1 Command the dog to "sit"; kneel beside it and hold its collar to restrain. Keep a treat in the other hand.

Food held in clenched fist to stop dog from snatching

2 Place the treat on the dog's nose and move it downward. As the dog sniffs the treat, move the treat forward in front of its nose and body.

Dog moves down to keep in touch with the treat

3 As you move the treat forward the dog should naturally start to stretch forward and lie down. Praise and reward it. Repeat the exercise until it responds to your words without a treat.

64 IF DOG WON'T LIE DOWN

With any early training, be it on or off the leash, expect to do quite a few practice runs, particularly with a puppy. If, after several practices, your dog still refuses to lie down, encourage it first into a begging position. Kneel down with the dog on your left side. Place your right palm under the dog's right foreleg, and then your left palm under its left foreleg. Now, raise it into a begging position. Gently lower the dog into either the "sphinx" or "flat" lying position. Keep calling its name and praising it.

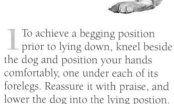

Gently hold the dog's legs. Do not grip them

1 To achieve a begging position prior to lying down, kneel beside the dog and position your hands comfortably, one under each of its forelegs. Reassure it with praise, and lower the dog into the lying postion.

2 Ease it to the ground by gently pressing on its body and pulling its legs forward. Keep the pressure on its shoulders for a few seconds once it lies down. Praise it, and on release say "okay." If it still jumps up to greet you, stop the praise, put it back in the lying position, and start again.

Keep fingers together over dog's shoulder muscles

65 How to Praise

A dog needs to be shown and reassured that it is responding correctly to commands. Food tidbits, toys, stroking its body, and verbal praise help you to reinforce this. If, in training, your dog does exactly what you want, do not hesitate to make a fuss over it.

△ Comforting Contact
Praise your dog by giving it long strokes along its body. Use the flat of your palm to make even strokes.

◁ Handheld Tasty Treats
Food held above a dog's nose will attract its attention quickly, especially if the dog is hungry.

66 Sensible Rewards

After a few training runs you will soon learn which snack or toy your dog responds to. Strap on a fanny pack during training sessions so you can pull out tidbits or toys without interrupting its learning.

RING TOY

DRIED FOOD   COOKIES   CHEW STICKS   THROW BALL   BONE TOY

67 PULLING ON THE LEASH

Pulling on the leash is the most common problem faced by dog owners. The remedy is to re-train (*see pp.44–9*) and command to heel (*see pp.52–5*). Don't try to match your strength against the dog since this may only incite it to pull even more.

EXCITED LEASH PULLING

1 ◁ Walk the dog on your left side, and hold the leash in both hands. As it pulls, slide your left hand down the leash and pull firmly.

Hands pull back once, firmly

Light jerks on leash bring dog into position

Give a small food reward each time it heels and sits without pulling

2 With your dog in the correct heel position, command it to sit. Start to walk again. Now try walking to heel (*see pp.52–3*).

3 Repeat the "heel" and "sit" procedure each time the dog pulls forward. When it starts to walk quietly to heel without pulling, reward it with a food treat and try it again.

68 HOW TO HEEL ON A LEASH

Teaching a dog to walk "to heel" is a key part of obedience training, and a prime duty for a dog owner when outdoors with a dog. Some owners like to start without a leash (*see pp.54–5*); whether you try first with or without a leash, keep reward snacks handy to reinforce your command.

1 ◁ Start the training indoors: kneel in front of the dog and let it smell a leash. Attach the leash to its collar and be sure not to apply any tension to the leash as yet.

4 ◁ When the dog heels, give it the tidbit. Keep eye contact and say its name and "good dog." Then give the command to sit and repeat the praise "good dog." Start to increase the distance as the dog obeys the sequence of heel commands.

Dog stays close to owner's legs

5 ▷ Now try a simple turn to the right. Guide the dog around to the right with your left hand and give the command "heel."

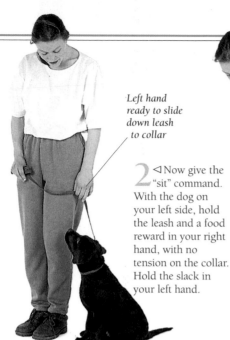

*Left hand
ready to slide
down leash
to collar*

2 ◁ Now give the "sit" command. With the dog on your left side, hold the leash and a food reward in your right hand, with no tension on the collar. Hold the slack in your left hand.

*Leash given
a quick jerk*

3 △ Begin to walk with the dog beside you, then give the command "heel." Pull back gently on the leash or collar if the dog surges forward.

6 ▷ To make a left turn, increase your own speed and hold a treat in front of the dog's nose to slow it down. Keep the dog close to your left leg, and give the command "steady" to help slow it down.

*Owner holds
dog back by
its collar*

*Dog is kept
close to your
legs at all
times*

69 HEEL WITHOUT A LEASH

When out walking with your dog it must always be under control. Training a dog to heel with a leash will help you insure that control, although it is also a delight to have your pet walking obediently by your side without a leash. Most dogs, especially from a young age, will naturally follow their owner, especially if there is the extra lure of a treat in sight. Keep food treats handy and make training sessions enjoyable, short, and frequent; no more than 15 minutes, up to four times a day. Practice in a quiet area, away from crowds if possible.

Keeping eye contact is crucial

1 △ Keep the dog on your left side and hold its collar with your left hand. Attract its attention by calling its name and showing it the tasty tidbit.

Owner repeats the "heel" command and says "good dog" to encourage it

Arm draws dog to the right, encouraging a turn

4 ▷ To encourage a right turn, bend your knees and hold the food near to the dog's nose. Make the right turn repeating the "heel" command as you do this. The dog will have to speed up to walk around you.

Dog's head follows the treat intently

Arm prevents dog from surging forward

Scent of food keeps dog on the move

3 △ Give the command "wait," and kneel to your dog's right side. Hold the snack low to discourage any jumping. Place your left hand, palm down, under its body, near to its hind legs, to prevent the dog from moving forward.

2 △ Walk in a straight line with the dog following the food reward. Give the command "heel." Keep your left hand low, and bend downward, ready to grasp the dog's collar.

Dog slows down as it receives reward

5 ▷ To make a left turn, use your left hand to guide the dog around by its collar while giving the command "steady." Hold a food reward low down and move your right hand to the left. The dog should follow the reward. Try several practice walks.

70 MEETING CHILDREN

Children are more at risk from bites because they are smaller and less imposing than adults. Explain to any child that wants to stroke your dog that some dogs can be unfriendly and that they must never rush up, shout, or pat the dog on its head. The dog should be introduced to children only in the presence, and under the supervision, of an adult. Allow the child to stroke the dog from the side, not the front. Praise the dog for its good behavior, but be ready to restrain it if it snaps or growls.

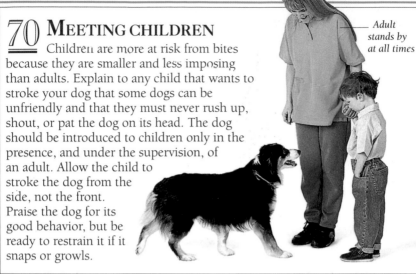

Adult stands by at all times

71 MEETING OTHER DOGS

Be cautious when your dog encounters another dog. Most dogs do get along with each other, but male territorial traits often lead to fights. Fighting is more likely with dogs of the same sex, size, and age. Avoid leash tension, and praise your dog for just sniffing other dogs and not showing any signs of aggression.

Taut leash encourages aggression

72 UNSAVORY EATING HABITS

Animal droppings can appear nourishing to dogs, and scavenging around horse droppings and the like is natural for some dogs such as the Golden Retriever. If you see your dog behaving in this way, first give the command "no." If it picks up the droppings say "drop." Surprise it with a water pistol or distract it with a toy to back up your command. A few dogs will eat their own (or even another dog's) droppings. To help prevent this bad habit, pick up stool promptly and keep the dog's environment free of stool.

73 A FIRM HAND

To reinforce your verbal commands, hand signals, and body language in general, it's useful to have a few backups to make sure your dog understands it is behaving badly or not responding to your authority. Plant sprays, water pistols, whistles, alarms, and toys are useful distractions to help you discipline a dog and say "no" or "stop it." Do not physically punish a dog for unwanted behavior. A dominant stance, stern words, and a squirt or whistle will suffice.

PLANT SPRAY

WATER PISTOL

ALARM

DISTRACTING TOY

PLAY TIME & EXERCISE

74 CHOOSE A CHEW TOY

Dogs enjoy chewing, chasing, and pulling, so make sure they play or exercise with a toy that you choose, rather than with a household item they fancy. A chewy bone exercises the jaws, while pulls are ideal for tug-of-war games. Balls and frisbees are fun for a dog to chase and retrieve.

RUBBER BALL   **NYLON BONE**   **DOG PULL**

75 SUITABLE TOYS

Toys for dogs are specifically designed to be safe and fun. Restrict the use of any toy to prevent possessiveness in your dog.

- Avoid balls or toys that could be easily destroyed and swallowed.
- Do not give old shoes or clothes. It will assume it can chew new ones.

76 MAKE A CHEW TOY

Insert cheese spread into hollow bone

A good alternative to ready-made toys is to get a hollow bone, make sure it is sterilized, and then insert cheese spread or paste into its core. Show the bone to your dog and tell it there is food inside, then place it on the floor. This is an ideal "home alone" toy, and your dog will get plenty of chewing practice trying to reach the food.

HOLLOW BONE

77 PLAY BALL & FRISBEE

Chasing after a flying frisbee or a bouncing ball makes terrific exercise and an exciting outdoor game for your dog. Insure that you have plenty of unrestricted space to allow as much exercise for your dog as possible. Catch-and-retrieve games are an excellent way to test your dog's reactions and obedience, channel its natural jumping instincts, reduce destructive activity, and help you to assert your authority.

CATCH-AND-RETRIEVE GAME

PLASTIC FRISBEE

78 TRY TUG-OF-WAR

Bored or inactive dogs are prone to bursts of destructive behavior. A tug-of-war game with a pull toy helps channel that energy into positive exercise. Make sure that you always win; otherwise, your dog will believe that it is dominant over you.

DROP BEFORE YOU TUG
Play tug-of-war only after your dog has learned how to drop an object on your command.

KNOTTED ROPE TUG TOY

79 EXERCISE DAILY

Once your dog has learned obedience training, you should take it out at least once a day for exercise on the leash, and let it off the leash to run in a permitted place. Take a ball or frisbee so you can encourage vigorous exercise in a controllable space and a short time.

◁ OFF THE LEASH
Allow vigorous exercise at least once a day, as well as frequent walks.

△ ON THE LEASH
An extendible leash allows safe exercise when other dogs are about.

80 JOG THE DOG

Training your dog to run to heel makes exercise rewarding and fun for you and your pet. If running in urban areas or along roads, take care and adhere to traffic rules. If you are exercising in the countryside, be sure your dog does not chase farm animals or run on cultivated land. This is when the walking-to-heel command is essential. If you are in doubt about your dog's obedience, it is best to keep it on a leash when you go out jogging.

Ensure the dog stays close by your side

TRAVEL & VACATIONS

DOG CARRIER

81 TAKE A DOG CARRIER

For air or car journeys, crate-trained dogs could go in their crate, if manageable. Otherwise you need a dog carrier, especially for small dogs. The carrier (*left*) has a carrying handle, locking catch, ventilation slits, rounded corners for easy cleaning, and plenty of room.

82 INSTALL A CAR GRILLE

You can buy special safety grilles that restrict dogs to the back of a station wagon or minivan. This prevents a dog from hurtling forward if you should have to stop suddenly, and helps to keep the upholstery in the rest of the car clean.

CAR SAFETY GRILLE

DOG SEATBELT

83 SEATBELTS FOR DOGS

You can have special seatbelts fitted for dogs that will greatly reduce the risk of your pet being injured in a car accident. A seatbelt is especially useful if you have a car for which a grille is not suitable. The other advantage of a seatbelt is that it prevents the dog from distracting you while you are driving. As an alternative, you could tie its leash, attached to its collar, onto a seatbelt anchor. This also prevents excess movement.

COVER THE SEAT

84 CAR TRIP TIPS

Take your dog on frequent, short trips to get it used to the car.
- Avoid feeding it before a journey.
- Cover the upholstery and floor with old newspapers or towels.
- Use a sunblind for hot, sunny days.
- Always take a large, plastic water container to quench a dog's thirst.
- Stop every two to three hours so your dog can have a good drink, get some exercise, and relieve itself.

85 STOP OVERHEATING

Dogs cannot lose heat by sweating: all they can do is pant. They will suffer from heatstroke and can die quickly from overheating. In summer or winter, a hot car is a death trap for dogs, so never leave a car unattended in warm weather, even in the shade with a window barely open, or with the heater running. Use a car sunblind to block out the sun. An obscured view also helps to calm excitable dogs.

SUNBLIND ON CAR WINDOW

APPLY COLD WATER FAST

86 IF IT OVERHEATS

Panting, salivation, and later collapse are the sure signs that a dog is overheated. Remove it from the hot spot immediately. Clear its mouth of saliva to ease breathing, and sponge the face with cool water. If possible, wrap the dog's body in a wet, but not ice-cold, towel. Pour cold water over the towel to prevent further warming. Allow the dog to drink.

87 WATER SAFETY

If you are taking your dog on a boating trip on the sea, a lake, or any open stretch of water a long way from shore, put a life jacket on it. Dogs can be excellent swimmers over short distances, but they can drown from exhaustion if they have to swim a long way. A life jacket will help the animal to stay buoyant if it accidentally falls in.

Dog life jacket helps it to float

88 HIKING HINT

If you are going on a lengthy hike you could buy special saddlebags that a dog will get used to carrying over long distances. The dog backpack can carry your pet's dish, food, and utensils. It is comfortable and has fasteners to secure it. Your dog must be physically fit before you embark on a hike.

BACKPACK

89 RABIES RISKS

Few areas are rabies-free, and those that are consist mainly of islands and peninsulas. Rabies is the most dangerous zoonosis; that is, a disease that can be transmitted from animal to animal, including man. Racoons, bats, skunks and foxes can be common carriers, and the virus is transmitted in saliva through bites. Personality change as well as excessive salivation are the warning signs. All dogs should be vaccinated against rabies in those areas where the disease occurs. In rabies-infected areas, humans at risk from dog bites should also be vaccinated.

90 QUARANTINE

If you are bringing a dog to a rabies-free country, you will be required to put your pet into special quarantined premises for many months. You must check this carefully well before embarking. Alternatively, you may be asked to prove that your dog was effectively vaccinated against rabies at least four months before your arrival. The costs mount up because approved quarantine premises are expensive and you also have to pay for port or airport carriage, airline handling, transportation, and vet insurance.

HEALTH CHECKS

91 GOOD HEALTH

You can do your own regular pet health checkup once a month (as shown here), but you should also book your dog for an annual medical examination with your vet.

TEETH AND GUMS
Check for bad breath, dribbling saliva, inflamed gums, and loose or broken teeth.

EYE WATCH
Look for bloodshot eyes and squinting.

ANAL AREA
Watch out for worms in feces, white grains on rear, or persistent diarrhea.

SKIN COMPLAINTS
Be aware of persistent scratching, sudden chewing or licking, redness, and increased hair loss.

SURE SIGNS OF CANINE HEALTH
Healthy dogs are vibrant and alert, though happy to lie down for much of the day.

EAR INFECTIONS
Check for head shaking, discharge in the ear canal, and swelling of the ear flap. A failure to respond to commands may be a sign of deafness.

PAWS AND PADS
Inspect the paws for cut or burned pads, and broken or damaged nails.

92 FLEAS

ADULT FLEA

Adult fleas live on your dog and contaminate the animal's enviroment with immature flea stages.

Look for black specks in your dog's coat called 'flea dirt'. Your vet can recommend effective flea control products like Revolution® (selamectin) to control fleas and prevent future flea infestations.

93 MITES & TICKS

If your pet has mites or ticks, ask your vet for help or you can bathe it with an appropriate insecticidal shampoo. Pull ticks off with tweezers right at the base of the skin, twisting the mouthpiece free.

MITE

TICK

LOUSE

94 WORM CHECK

Regular worming of your dog should control most internal parasites. Some worms require special medicines, but your vet will diagnose this and advise on the more severe infestations.

△ **TAPEWORM**
Watch for rice-like eggs around anus or movement in feces.

◁ **ROUNDWORM**
An off-white, earthwormlike parasite visible in the feces.

95 FIRST AID KIT

All dog owners would be advised to have a basic first aid kit, the contents of which (*see right*) should assist in reducing a dog's pain and distress, as well as help to prevent the situation from worsening while you contact the vet.

TAPE

GAUZE

STRONG BOX

SCISSORS

COTTON BALLS

DISINFECTANT

MUZZLE

96 BITE TREATMENT

The neck, face, ears, and chest are the body parts where dogs most commonly bite each other. If your dog has been in a fight, allow time for it to calm down before you examine it. Canine teeth make clean bites, so look for soft-tissue damage under the skin. A deep wound will probably have to be treated by a vet. (The safest way to separate fighting dogs is to pour water on them from a bucket or spray with a hose.)

1 If the skin is punctured, you must go to a vet for antibiotics. But first clip the fur away from the wound: fur in the wound can lead to trapped infection.

2 Carefully bathe the infected region with soap and rinse thoroughly with warm water. You may need to repeat cleaning and rinsing with water several times to get the wound clean.

3 If the dog's skin is lacerated rather than punctured, the wound should be thoroughly cleaned. Your vet may provide you with a topical treatment you can apply. Expect some bruising to become visible later on. See your vet immediately if the wound becomes red or drains cloudy fluid.

97 STING RELIEF

Wasp, hornet, and bee stings are common and cause pain and swelling. The usual sites for these stings are the face and mouth. Like humans, some dogs can be allergic to stings and react badly. If there is acute swelling to the mouth and throat, urgent vet care will be needed.

DRAW OUT A BEE STING WITH TWEEZERS

98 GIVING TABLETS

Some dogs can be devious about keeping pills in their mouths, and spitting them out later. If your pet does this, a good counter-trick is to try hiding the tablet in a chunk of meat, or a piece of bread, or even coat the pill in melted cheese.

1 △ Go to your dog; do not ask it to come to you. With one hand, open its mouth gently, and with the other drop the tablet well down the tongue.

2 ▷ Hold the dog's mouth firmly closed and hold its head up slightly. Stroke its throat and wait for it to swallow and lick its lips. Then praise it for swallowing.

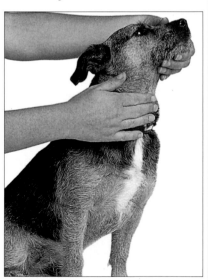

99 HEARTWORM

Canine heartworm has been diagnosed in all 50 states and in many countries around the globe. Adult heartworms are long white worms (up to about 12 inches) that live in the large blood vessels of the lungs as well as within the right side of the heart. Male and female worms mate to produce immature worms called microfilaria that circulate in bloodstream. Veterinarians routinely identify dogs with heartworm by performing blood tests that detect a substance within the female worm (heartworm antigen) or by finding microfilaria in the bloodstream.

Heartworm is transmitted to dogs by the bite of mosquitoes that carry infectious immature worms. Mosquitoes become infected when they feed on dogs carrying microfilaria and when mosquitoes are exposed to proper environmental conditions. It takes about 6 months for adult heartworms to develop in dogs following the bite of an infected mosquito. Adult worms can damage the lung's blood vessels, heart, or secondarily damage other body organs. Dogs with heartworm may cough, tire easily, or develop heart failure and die although not every infected dog will show clinical signs of illness even though they may harbor many adult worms.

Mosquito becomes infected while feeding on a heartworm infected dog

Mosquito transmits heartworm to uninfected dogs while feeding

Immature heartworms migrate to the heart and lungs where they develop into adults and cause disease

Revolution® (selamectin) is a convenient topical medication that is administered at the base of the neck in front of your dog's shoulder blades every 30 days and prevents heartworm as well as fleas and other harmful parasites. Your veterinarian is the best person to discuss the prevention, diagnosis or treatment of heartworm and he or she can recommend a preventative protocol that will assure your dog will be protected against this all too common and serious parasite.

100 STRETCHER FOR AN INJURED DOG

If your dog is in a traffic accident, do not panic. Use a blanket or coat as a stretcher to remove it carefully from the source of danger.

- Muzzle it with a scarf or bandage.
- Look for bleeding, distorted limbs.
- Do not handle a fractured limb.
- Get someone to help you lift it.

1 Once you have checked the dog's condition, try to get someone to help you to support its weight and lift it onto a blanket or coat. Avoid touching injuries.

2 Lift very gently and carry it to a car to go to the vet. If on your own, place the coat along the dog's back and drag it by the neck and hips onto the "stretcher."

101 WHEN TO VISIT THE VET

Every dog-owner should take his or her pet to a vet for a medical checkup at least once a year. If the animal is in an accident, even with no obvious injury or bleeding, take it at once for urgent veterinary help. Many vets are linked to a 24-hour emergency service. Your dog may have internal injuries or fractures, which only a professional can diagnose. Visit the office also:

- For expert dietary assistance.
- For the best breeding advice.
- If your dog staggers or falls over.
- If blood is present or dog vomits.
- If in acute pain/abnormal swelling.

Using a stethoscope to check breathing

INDEX

ACKNOWLEDGMENTS

Dorling Kindersley would like to thank Hilary Bird for compiling the index,
Ann Kay for proofreading, Murdo Culver for design assistance, and Mark
Bracey for computer assistance.

Photography
KEY: t top; b bottom; c center; l left; r right; tl top left; tr top right; bl bottom left;
All photographs by Andy Crawford, Steve Gorton, Tim Ridley,
except for: Jane Burton 12–13, 15t, 72; Guide Dogs for the Blind
Association 9tl; Dave King 3, 7, 8bl, 11, 61b; Tracy Morgan 10t;
Stephen Oliver 21t, 24b; Steve Shott 1, 29b, 30b, 66t; David Ward
8tr, 9b, 10b, 21b, 56b, 60tl; Jerry Young 14 bl.

Illustrations
Rowan Clifford 66, 67, 69; Chris Forsey 63, 65;
Janos Marffy 38.

revolution
(selamectin)

NADA 141-152, Approved by FDA
REVOLUTION® (selamectin)

Topical Parasiticide For Dogs and Cats

CAUTION:
US Federal law restricts this drug to use by or on the order of a licensed veterinarian.

DESCRIPTION:
Revolution (selamectin) Topical Parasiticide is available as a colorless to yellow, ready to use solution in single dose tubes for topical (dermal) treatment of dogs six weeks of age and older and cats eight weeks of age and older. The content of each tube is formulated to provide a minimum of 2.7 mg/lb (6 mg/kg) of body weight of selamectin. The chemical composition of selamectin is (5Z,25S)-25-cyclohexyl-4'-O-de(2,6-dideoxy-3-O-methyl-α-L-arabino-hexopyranosyl)-5-demethoxy-25-de (1-methylpropyl)-22,23-dihydro-5-hydroxyiminoavermectin A_{1a}.

INDICATIONS:
Revolution is recommended for use in dogs six weeks of age or older and cats eight weeks of age and older for the following parasites and indications:

Dogs:
Revolution kills adult fleas and prevents flea eggs from hatching for one month and is indicated for the prevention and control of flea infestations (Ctenocephalides felis), prevention of heartworm disease caused by Dirofilaria immitis, and the treatment and control of ear mite (Otodectes cynotis) infestations. Revolution also is indicated for the treatment and control of sarcoptic mange (Sarcoptes scabiei) and for the control of tick infestations due to Dermacentor variabilis.

Cats:
Revolution kills adult fleas and prevents flea eggs from hatching for one month and is indicated for the prevention and control of flea infestations (Ctenocephalides felis), prevention of heartworm disease caused by Dirofilaria immitis, and the treatment and control of ear mite (Otodectes cynotis) infestations. Revolution is also indicated for the treatment and control of roundworm (Toxocara cati) and intestinal hookworm (Ancylostoma tubaeforme) infections in cats.

WARNINGS:
Not for human use. Keep out of the reach of children. In humans, Revolution may be irritating to skin and eyes. Reactions such as hives, itching and skin redness have been reported in humans in rare instances. Individuals with known hypersensitivity to Revolution should use the product with caution or consult a health care professional. Revolution contains isopropyl alcohol and the preservative butylated hydroxytoluene (BHT). Wash hands after use and wash off any product in contact with the skin immediately with soap and water. If contact with eyes occurs, then flush eyes copiously with water. In case of ingestion by a human, contact a physician immediately. The material safety data sheet (MSDS) provides more detailed occupational safety information. For a copy of the MSDS or to report adverse reactions attributable to exposure to this product, call 1-888-963-8471.

Flammable - Keep away from heat, sparks, open flames or other sources of ignition.

Do not use in sick, debilitated or underweight animals (see SAFETY).

PRECAUTIONS:
Prior to administration of Revolution, dogs should be tested for existing heartworm infections. At the discretion of the veterinarian, infected dogs should be treated to remove adult heartworms. Revolution is not effective against adult D. immitis and, while the number of circulating microfilariae may decrease following treatment, Revolution is not effective for microfilariae clearance. Hypersensitivity reactions have not been observed in dogs with patent heartworm infections administered three times the recommended dose of Revolution. Higher doses were not tested.

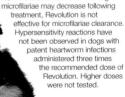

ADVERSE REACTIONS:

Pre-approval clinical trials:

Following treatment with Revolution, transient localized alopecia with or without inflammation at or near the site of application was observed in approximately 1% of 691 treated cats. Other signs observed rarely (≤0.5% of 1743 treated cats and dogs) included vomiting, loose stool or diarrhea with or without blood, anorexia, lethargy, salivation, tachypnea, and muscle tremors.

Post-approval experience:

In addition to the aforementioned clinical signs that were reported in pre-approval clinical trials, there have been reports of pruritus, urticaria, erythema, ataxia, fever, and rare reports of death. There have also been rare reports of seizures in dogs (see **WARNINGS**).

DOSAGE:

The recommended minimum dose is 2.7 mg selamectin per pound (6 mg/kg) of body weight.

Administer the entire contents of a single dose tube (or two tubes used in combination for dogs weighing over 130 pounds) of Revolution topically in accordance with the following tables. (See **ADMINISTRATION** for the recommended treatment intervals.)

Cats (lb)	Package color	mg per tube	Potency (mg/mL)	Administered volume (mL)
Up to 5	Mauve	15 mg	60	0.25
5.1–15	Blue	45 mg	60	0.75

For cats over 22 lbs use the appropriate combination of tubes.

Dogs (lb)	Package color	mg per tube	Potency (mg/mL)	Administered volume (mL)
Up to 5	Mauve	15 mg	60	0.25
5.1–10	Purple	30 mg	120	0.25
10.1–20	Brown	60 mg	120	0.5
20.1–40	Red	120 mg	120	1.0
40.1–85	Teal	240 mg	120	2.0
85.1–130	Plum	360 mg	120	3.0

For dogs over 130 lbs use the appropriate combination of tubes.

Recommended for use in dogs 6 weeks of age and older and in cats 8 weeks of age and older.

ADMINISTRATION:

A veterinarian or veterinary technician should demonstrate or instruct the pet owner regarding the appropriate technique for applying Revolution topically to dogs and cats prior to first use.

Firmly press the cap down to puncture the seal on the Revolution tube; a clicking sound will confirm that the cap has successfully punctured the seal. Remove the cap and check to ensure that the tip of the tube is open. To administer the product, part the hair on the back of the animal at the base of the neck in front of the shoulder blades until the skin is visible. Place the tip of the tube on the skin and squeeze the tube 3 or 4 times to empty its entire contents directly onto the skin in one spot. Keeping the tube squeezed, drag it away from the liquid and lift to remove. Check the tube to ensure that it is empty. Do not massage the product into the skin. Due to alcohol content, do not apply to broken skin. Avoid contact between the product and fingers. Do not apply when the haircoat is wet. Bathing or shampooing the animal 2 or more hours after treatment will not reduce the effectiveness

of Revolution. Stiff hair, clumping of hair, hair discoloration, or a slight powdery residue may be observed at the treatment site in some animals. These effects are temporary and do not affect the safety or effectiveness of the product. Discard empty tubes in your ordinary household refuse.

Flea Control in Dogs and Cats

For the prevention and control of flea infestations, Revolution should be administered at monthly intervals throughout the flea season, starting one month before fleas become active. In controlled laboratory studies >98% of fleas were killed within 36 hours. Results of clinical field studies using Revolution monthly demonstrated >90% control of flea infestations within 30 days of the first dose. Dogs and cats treated with Revolution, including those with pre-existing flea allergy dermatitis, showed improvement in clinical signs associated with fleas as a direct result of eliminating the fleas from the animals and their environment.

If the dog or cat is already infested with fleas when the first dose of Revolution is administered, adult fleas on the animal are killed and no viable fleas hatch from eggs after the first administration. However, an environmental infestation of fleas may persist for a short time after beginning treatment with Revolution because of the emergence of adult fleas from pupae.

Heartworm Prevention in Dogs and Cats

For the prevention of heartworm disease, Revolution must be administered on a monthly basis. Revolution may be administered year-round or at least within one month after the animal's first exposure to mosquitoes and monthly thereafter until the end of the mosquito season. The final dose must be given within one month after the last exposure to mosquitoes. If a dose is missed and a monthly interval between dosing is exceeded then immediate administration of Revolution and resumption of monthly dosing will minimize the opportunity for the development of adult heartworms. When replacing another heartworm preventive product in a heartworm disease prevention program, the first dose of Revolution must be given within a month of the last dose of the former medication.

Selamectin, the active ingredient in Revolution, is a macrocyclic lactone compound. These compounds effectively prevent the development of adult heartworms when administered to dogs and cats within one month of exposure to infective (L3) *Dirofilaria immitis* larvae. Efficacy of macrocyclic lactones decreases below 100% in dogs, however, if first administered >2 months after exposure to infective larvae. Thus, in heartworm endemic regions, delaying initiation of heartworm prevention using Revolution beyond 2 months of first exposure to infective larvae (e.g., starting puppies and kittens at >8 weeks of age), or gaps of >2 months in the administration of Revolution during periods of heartworm transmission, increases the risk of the animal acquiring heartworms. Animals with unknown heartworm history that test negative for heartworms prior to the initiation of Revolution may be harboring pre-patent infections at the time Revolution was started. Testing such animals 3–4 months after initiation of Revolution would be necessary to confirm their negative heartworm status.

At the discretion of the veterinarian, cats ≥6 months of age may be tested to determine the presence of existing heartworm infections before beginning treatment with Revolution. Cats already infected with adult heartworms can be given Revolution monthly to prevent further infections.

Ear Mite Treatment in Dogs and Cats
For the treatment of ear mite (*O. cynotis*) infestations in dogs and cats, Revolution should be administered once as a single topical dose. A second monthly dose may be required in some dogs. Monthly use of Revolution will control any subsequent ear mite infestations. In the clinical field trials ears were not cleaned, and many animals still had debris in their ears after the second dose. Cleansing of the infested ears is recommended to remove the debris.

Sarcoptic Mange Treatment in Dogs
For the treatment of sarcoptic mange (*S. scabiei*) in dogs, Revolution should be administered once as a single topical dose. A second monthly dose may be required in some dogs. Monthly use of Revolution will control any subsequent sarcoptic mange mite infestations. Because of the difficulty in finding sarcoptic mange mites on skin scrapings, effectiveness assessments also were based on resolution of clinical signs. Resolution of the pruritus associated with the mite infestations was observed in approximately 50% of the dogs 30 days after the first treatment and in approximately 90% of the dogs 30 days after the second monthly treatment.

Tick Control in Dogs
For the control of tick (*Dermacentor variabilis*) infestations in dogs, Revolution should be administered on a monthly basis. In heavy tick infestations, complete efficacy may not be achieved after the first dose. In these cases, one additional dose may be administered two weeks after the previous dose, with monthly dosing continued thereafter.

Nematode Treatment in Cats
For the treatment and control of intestinal hookworm (*A. tubaeforme*) and roundworm (*T. cati*) infections, Revolution should be applied once as a single topical dose.

SAFETY:
Revolution has been tested safe in over 100 different pure and mixed breeds of healthy dogs and over 15 different pure and mixed breeds of healthy cats, including pregnant and lactating females, breeding males and females, puppies six weeks of age and older, kittens eight weeks of age and older, and avermectin-sensitive collies. A kitten, estimated to be 5–6 weeks old (0.3 kg), died 8 1/2 hours after receiving a single treatment of Revolution at the recommended dosage. The kitten displayed clinical signs which included muscle spasms, salivation and neurological signs. The kitten was a stray with an unknown history and was malnourished and underweight (see **WARNINGS**).

DOGS: In safety studies, Revolution was administered at 1, 3, 5, and 10 times the recommended dose to six-week-old puppies, and no adverse reactions were observed. The safety of Revolution administered orally also was tested in case of accidental oral ingestion. Oral administration of Revolution at the recommended topical dose in 5- to 8-month-old beagles did not cause any adverse reactions. In a pre-clinical study selamectin was dosed orally to ivermectin-sensitive collies. Oral administration of 2.5, 10, and 15 mg/kg in this dose escalating study did not cause any adverse reactions; however, eight hours after receiving 5 mg/kg orally, one avermectin-sensitive collie became ataxic for several hours, but did not show any other adverse reactions after receiving subsequent doses of 10 and 15 mg/kg orally. In a topical safety study conducted with avermectin-sensitive collies at 1, 3 and 5 times the recommended dose of Revolution, salivation was observed in all treatment groups, including the vehicle control. Revolution also was administered at 3 times the recommended dose to heartworm infected dogs, and no adverse effects were observed.

CATS: In safety studies, Revolution was applied at 1, 3, 5, and 10 times the recommended dose to six-week-old kittens. No adverse reactions were observed. The safety of Revolution administered orally also was tested in case of accidental oral ingestion. Oral administration of the recommended topical dose of Revolution to cats caused salivation and intermittent vomiting. Revolution also was applied at 4 times the recommended dose to patent heartworm infected cats, and no adverse reactions were observed.

In well-controlled clinical studies, Revolution was used safely in animals receiving other frequently used veterinary products such as vaccines, anthelmintics, antiparasitics, antibiotics, steroids, collars, shampoos and dips.

STORAGE CONDITIONS: Store below 30°C (86°F).

HOW SUPPLIED: Available in eight separate dose strengths for dogs and cats of different weights (see **DOSAGE**). Revolution for puppies and kittens is available in cartons containing 3 single dose tubes. Revolution for cats and dogs is available in cartons containing 3 or 6 single dose tubes.

zoetis
Distributed by:
Zoetis Inc.
Kalamazoo, MI 49007

www.revolutionpet.com

10309504